What is Air?

by Megan McDonald

Glenview, Illinois
Boston, Massachusetts
Chandler, Arizona
New York, New York

Photographs

Every effort has been made to secure permission and provide appropriate credit for photographic material. The publisher deeply regrets any omission and pledges to correct errors called to its attention in subsequent editions.

Photo locators denoted as follows: Top (T), Center (C), Bottom (B), Left (L), Right (R), Background (Bkgd).

CVR: Topseller/Shutterstock; 1: Antonvp1972/Fotolia; 2: Andy Crawford/Dorling Kindersley Ltd.; 3: Andy Crawford/ Dorling Kindersley Ltd.; 4: Sergey Novikov/123RF; 5T: Clive Streeter/Dorling Kindersley Ltd.; 5B: Peter Chadwick/Dorling Kindersley Ltd.; 6: FloridaStock/Shutterstock; 7: Topseller/Shutterstock; 8: Andy Crawford/Dorling Kindersley Ltd.; 8-9Bkgd: Brian Cosgrove/Dorling Kindersley Ltd.; 9: James Jackson/Dorling Kindersley Ltd.; 10: Philip Gatward/Dorling Kindersley Ltd.; 11: Alexander Gordeyev/Shutterstock; 12: Dorling Kindersley Ltd.; 13: Susan Stevenson/Fotolia; 15: Dima Fadeev/Shutterstock; FP5: Sergey Novikov/123RF

ISBN-13: 978-0-328-61778-4
ISBN-10: 0-328-61778-4

8 16

What You Already Know

A property is something you can observe with your senses. Objects have many different properties. Size, color, shape, and feel are all properties. Weight is also a property. Weight is how heavy an object feels when you pick it up. Some objects weigh more than other objects.

Some things are solids. Some things are liquids. Some things are gases. Solids, liquids, and gases are different from one another.

A solid has its own size and shape. When a solid is moved, it does not change shape.

A liquid takes the shape of its container. It has its own size, but not its own shape. Liquids can be poured. One kind of liquid is water. You can put liquid in a measuring cup. It will show the size of a liquid.

A gas does not have its own size. A gas does not have its own shape. It takes the size and shape of its container. You cannot see most gases.

You are about to read more about one gas. Air is a gas, and it is all around us.

What is air?

Air is a gas. It is all around us. Air is touching us all the time. We cannot see air, but sometimes we can feel it. Have you ever felt the wind on your skin? That is air.

An air-filled balloon weighs more than an empty balloon.

We can also see what air does around us. The wind can carry a kite. It can make trees sway. When you blow up a balloon, you are filling it with air. Now the balloon takes up more space and weighs more.

Rising Air

Hot air is lighter than cool air. Air that is warm rises up. People can use hang gliders to soar through the air. Birds, such as eagles and sea gulls, soar on rising waves of air. The warm air keeps the birds' bodies lifted. Birds that glide have big wings so they can catch as much air as possible.

An eagle rides on a wave of warm air.

Hot air balloons make use of warm, rising air.

A hot air balloon can float because it has warm air in it. The bag of air is heated by a burner under the balloon. As the air in the bag cools, the balloon slowly starts to go down.

Moisture in Air

Air has moisture in it. This moisture is called water vapor. Water vapor is water that has turned into a gas. Warm air and water vapor rise. Then they cool. When air cools, the water vapor in it condenses to form clouds. Moisture from clouds is frozen when it begins to fall. If the air is warm, it changes to rain. When the clouds become heavy enough, the water falls to the ground as rain. This is called precipitation.

Rain and snow are kinds of precipitation.

Snow is another kind of precipitation. Water droplets in clouds turn into snowflakes when the air is below freezing. Snow has a lot of air trapped in it. This is why snow looks white.

Air Resistance

Air resistance slows down objects moving through air. You can feel air resistance when you ride a bike fast. It feels like the air is pushing against you.

Air resistance helps these parachutes fall gently to the ground.

Air resistance helps people land using parachutes. It slows them down as they fall through the air.

Cars and planes havc special shapes so they have less air resistance. People do not want cars and planes to be slowed down by air.

Air Pressure

Air presses down on objects around it. This is called air pressure. Air pressure gets less strong the higher we go. This is because there is less air. We are so used to the air pushing against us that we do not even feel it!

The air in these bicycle tires is under pressure.

Air is springy. It pushes back when you squash it. You can feel the pressure of air when you squeeze a ball or a bicycle tire. The air is pushed into a smaller space and feels tight. When you let go, the ball or tire will spring out again.

Some machines work using air pressure. This drill uses air pressure to help it make holes.

This drill uses the strong force of air under pressure.

Air Is Important

Air is an important gas. It is all around us. Its pressure is always pushing down on us. We cannot see it, but we can see and feel what it does. Warm rising air lets birds fly. Moisture in the air causes precipitation. You can feel air resistance when you go fast.

People can use air for many things. It lets hot air ballons and hang gliders fly. Windsurfers use it to move across the water. It slows down parachutes. It can even make drills work better. Air is amazing!

Glossary

air pressure   air pressing down on objects around it

air resistance   air slowing down objects moving through it

condenses   changes from water vapor to liquid water

precipitation   water that falls to the ground as rain, snow, or hail

water vapor   water that has turned into a gas